STORIES IN THE STARS

THE STORY OF THE GREAT BEAR

By Ingrid Griffin

Gareth Stevens
PUBLISHING

leveled reader science

Please visit our website, www.garethstevens.com. For a free color catalog of all our high-quality books, call toll free 1-800-542-2595 or fax 1-877-542-2596.

Library of Congress Cataloging-in-Publication Data

Griffin, Ingrid.
The story of the great bear / by Ingrid Griffin.
p. cm. — (Stories in the stars)
Includes index.
ISBN 978-1-4824-2665-6 (pbk.)
ISBN 978-1-4824-2666-3 (6 pack)
ISBN 978-1-4824-2667-0 (library binding)
1. Ursa Major — Juvenile literature. 2. Constellations — Juvenile literature. 3. Stars — Mythology — Juvenile literature. I. Title.
QB801.7 G754 2016
398.20937—d23

Published in 2016 by
Gareth Stevens Publishing
111 East 14th Street, Suite 349
New York, NY 10003

Designer: Nicholas Domiano
Editor: Therese Shea

Photo credits: Cover, p. 1 (bear) Dorling Kindersley/Getty Images; cover, p. 1 (stars) nienora/Shutterstock.com; pp. 5, 15 angelinast/Shutterstock.com; p. 7 Heritage Images/Hulton Fine Art Collection/Getty Images; p. 9 Print Collector/Hulton Archive/Getty Images; p. 11 Hill Street Studios/L Paul Verhage/Blend Images/Getty Images; p. 13 PHAS/Universal Images Group/Getty Images; p. 17 Miao Liao/Shutterstock.com; p. 19 Pi-Lens/Shutterstock.com; p. 21 Lisa Zador/Photodisc/Getty Images.

Printed in the United States of America

CPSIA compliance information: Batch #CS15GS: For further information contact Gareth Stevens, New York, New York at 1-800-542-2595.

CONTENTS

Boldface words appear in the glossary.

Bear in the Sky

A constellation is a group of stars that forms a shape. One constellation is called Ursa Major. That's Latin for "Great Bear." The constellation looks a bit like a bear. Many **cultures** have stories about the Great Bear in the sky.

5

Callisto

Ancient Greeks told a story about a beautiful **nymph** Callisto (kuh-LIH-stoh). The king of the gods, Zeus (ZOOS), fell in love with her. Callisto had a baby named Arcas (AHR-kuhs). Zeus's wife, Hera, was angry. She turned Callisto into a bear.

Callisto
Zeus

For years, Callisto hid from hunters. One day, she saw her son Arcas in a forest. She forgot she was a bear and ran to him. Arcas was scared. He took out a **spear** to kill the beast.

Zeus saw this happening. Quickly, he turned Arcas into a bear. Then, he threw both bears into the sky. They became constellations. Callisto became the Great Bear, or Ursa Major. Arcas became the constellation called the Little Bear, or Ursa Minor.

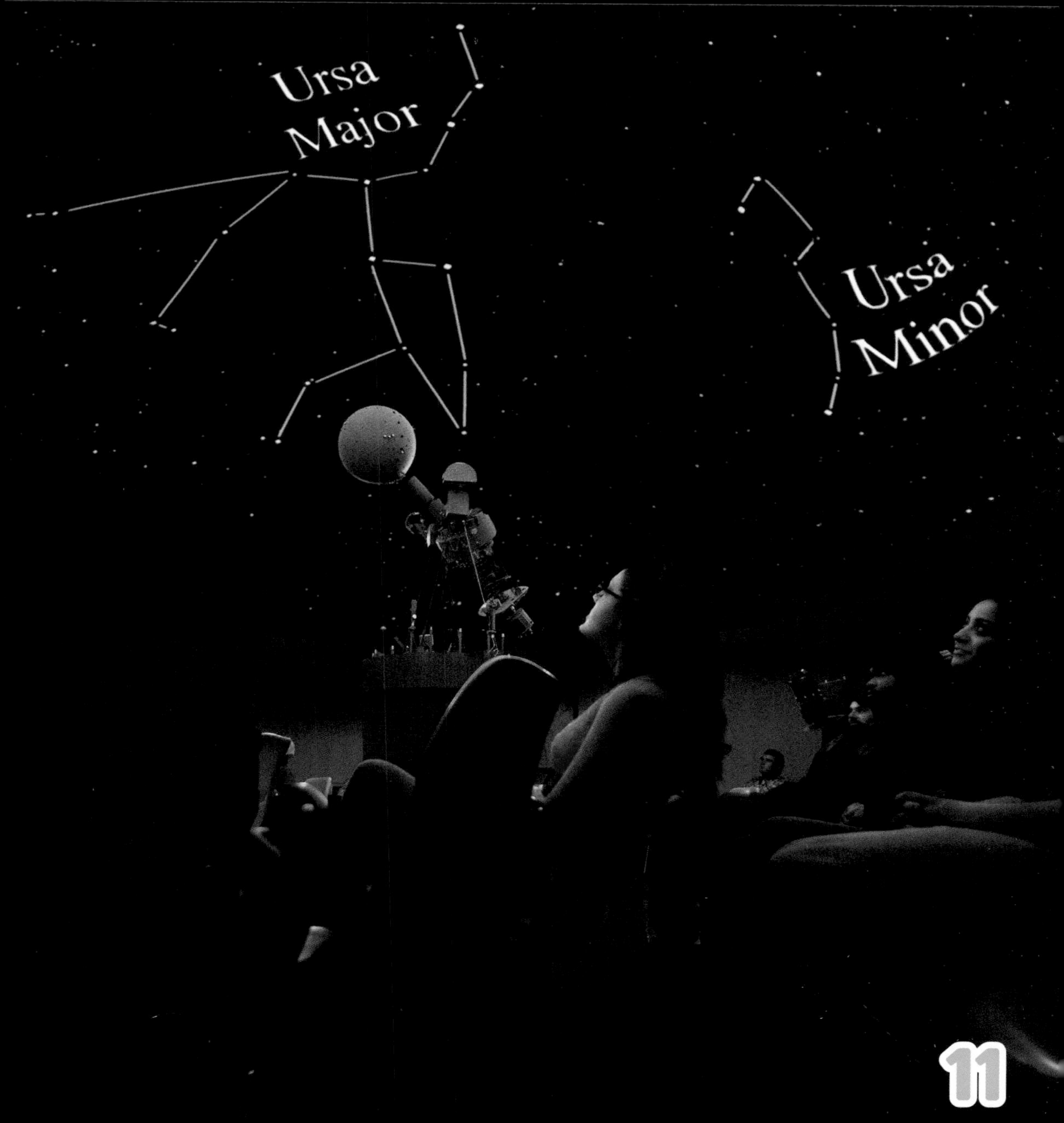

Ursa Major

Ursa Minor

Adrasteia

Another Greek story says the constellation is a tree nymph named Adrasteia (uh-DRAS-tee-uh). When Zeus was born, his father tried to kill him. His mother took him to an island where Adrasteia cared for him. Zeus later changed her into the Great Bear.

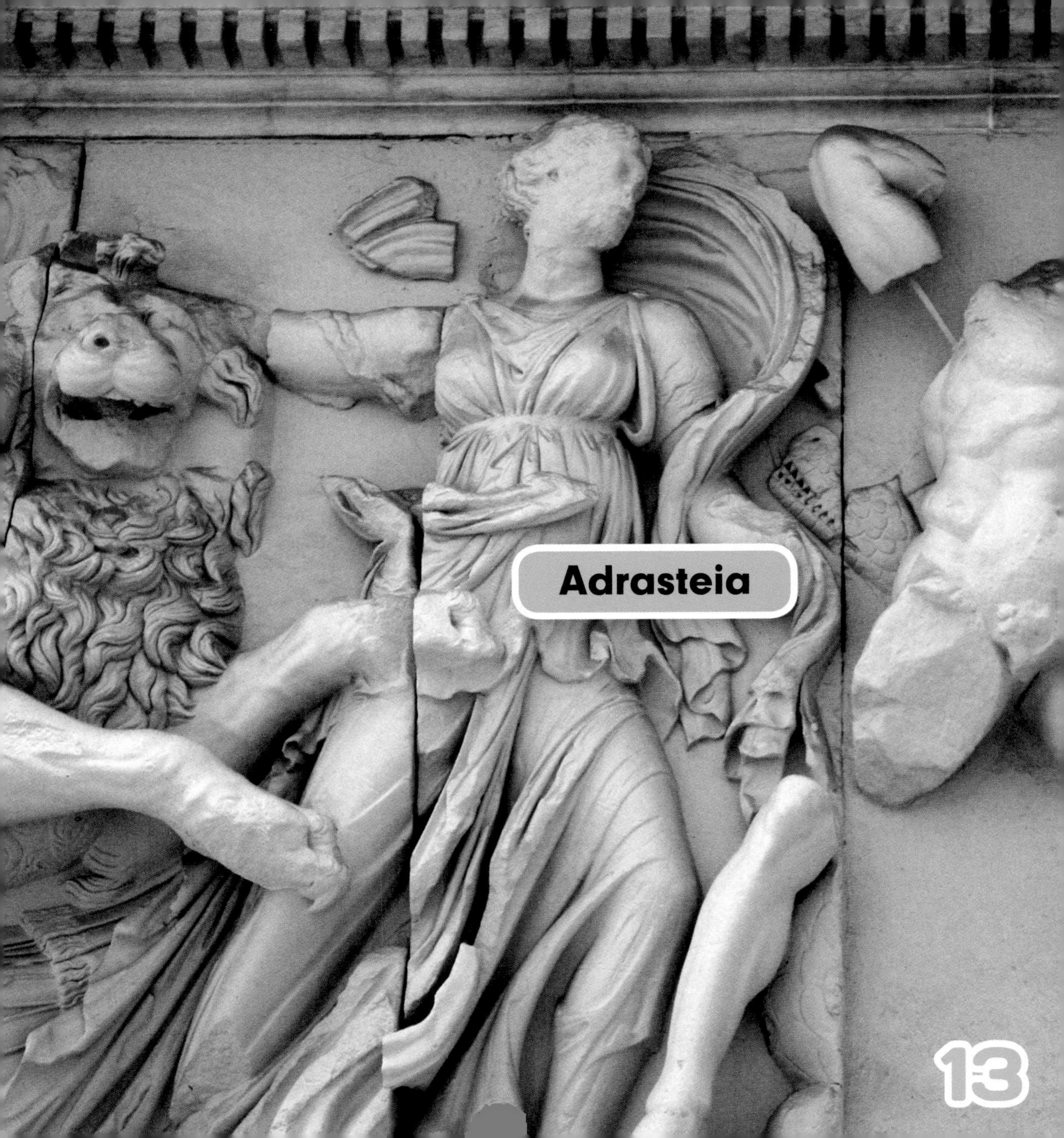
Adrasteia

The Big Dipper

Seven stars within the Great Bear constellation are called the Big Dipper. Their shape looks like a big spoon. The handle is the Great Bear's tail, and the cup is its hip. The Big Dipper isn't a constellation. It's called an **asterism** (AA-stuh-rih-zuhm).

Native American stories say the cup of the Big Dipper is a bear. The stars that make the handle are hunters chasing it. The Big Dipper is low in the sky during fall. It's said to make the leaves turn red.

The Big Dipper is easy to spot in the sky. In the days of slavery in the United States, some slaves escaped to safety by following the Big Dipper. They knew they were headed north if they followed its stars.

What Do You See?

Other cultures thought the Great Bear and the Big Dipper looked like a camel, shark, skunk, or boat. Ancient Romans thought it looked like a wagon pulled by oxen. Next time you're looking at the night sky, find pictures in the stars!

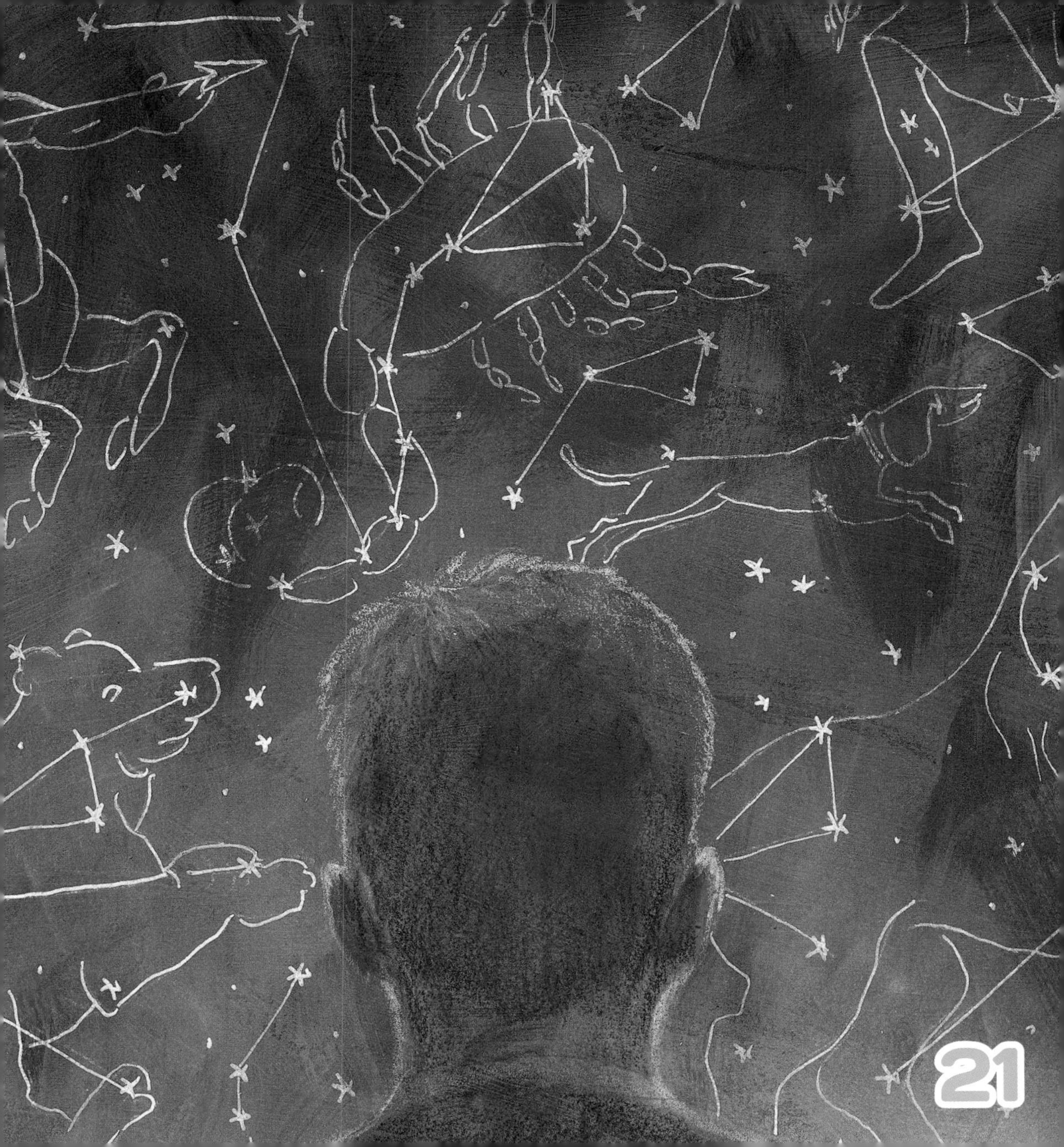

GLOSSARY

ancient: coming from a time long past

asterism: a small group of stars that forms a pattern

culture: a people who have their own beliefs and ways of life

nymph: in stories, a spirit in the shape of a young woman who lives in nature

spear: a long and pointed tool that is thrown in order to harm something

FOR MORE INFORMATION

BOOKS

Hoena, B. A. *Everything Mythology*. Washington, DC: National Geographic, 2014.

Meister, Cari. *The Story of Ursa Major and Ursa Minor: A Roman Constellation Myth*. North Mankato, MN: Picture Window Books, 2013.

Owings, Lisa. *The Constellation Ursa Major: The Story of the Big Bear*. Mankato, MN: Child's World, 2013.

WEBSITES

Ursa Major
starryskies.com/The_sky/constellations/ursa_major.html
Read more stories from different cultures about the Great Bear.

Ursa Major Constellation
www.solarsystemquick.com/universe/ursa-major-constellation.htm
Read quick facts about the famous constellation.

INDEX